This book is dedicate to my father
Late Mr. Sujauddin Kazi

Copyright Page

Corporate Sweet & Salt © Copyright 2020, Dr Nikhat M Hamza

All rights reserved. No part of this publication may be reproduced, distributed or transmitted in any form or by any means, including photocopying, recording, or other electronic or mechanical methods, without the prior written permission of the author, except in the case of brief quotations embodied in critical reviews and certain other non-commercial uses permitted by copyright law.

Although the author and publisher have made every effort to ensure that the information in this book was correct at press time, the author and publisher do not assume and hereby disclaim any liability to any party for any loss, damage, or disruption caused by errors or omissions, whether such errors or omissions result from negligence, accident, or any other cause.

Adherence to all applicable laws and regulations, including international, state and local governing professional licensing, business practices, advertising, and all other aspects of doing business in India or any other jurisdiction is the sole responsibility of the reader and consumer.

Neither the author nor the publisher assumes any responsibility or liability whatsoever on behalf of the consumer or reader of this material. Any perceived slight of any individual or organization is purely unintentional.

The resources in this book are provided for informational purposes only and should not be used to replace the specialized training and professional judgments.

Neither the author nor the publisher can be held responsible for the use of the information provided within this book.

Table Of Contents:

Preface

Inside

Dedication

Introduction

Chapter 1

Stages of organization

Chapter 2

Human nature and organization politics

Chapter 3

Diversity in the organization

Chapter 4

Employees generating Toxic work atmosphere

Chapter 5

A Wrong Man in Workers' Wonderland

Chapter 6

Leadership Intervention

Chapter 7

Role of Human Resource

About the Author

References

Preface

We are often unaware of the happiness we get during our college years as the mind is engrossed in the future. We only come to apprehend the importance of those jiffies once we leave college and join the professional lifecycle. This tendency underscores human nature, which directs people to give precedence to either the past or the future, at the expense of the present.

This book is close to my heart and dedicated to my father as it documents my professional life, which started prematurely due to the sudden demise of my parents. I desire to share the story of the people who made me who I am today. Like every daughter, I was very close to my dad. He was, and still is, my guide, philosopher, teacher, and hero. It is often said that a girl's heart desire is to marry a man who emulates her father's personality. I beg to differ with this proposition because nobody can ever take the place of my dad.

I would like to share with the reader of this book a myriad of unforgettable moments that always keep me attached to my parents. I am sure everyone has such memories, spanning between childhood and college life. Besides, experts argue that recalling striking moments with one's parents and friends reduces corporate stress.

After returning from school, and whenever I was at home, I used to spend much of my time with my father. Even though he had a car and a driver, I still used to pick him up from the office, without fail. You must be wondering how? I made it a habit to ride my beloved cycle to his workplace, just to see him emerge from the office and make him get into his car. Then, I would trail dad's car all the way home. His friends used to call me "bodyguard." Rather than get offended, I used to dismiss their label with a smile.

After retiring from the Army, my dad took up a job at an MNC company, where he worked as the chief of security for all the branches. My daily trips to this company taught me several life lessons. Since I was not allowed into the company's premises, I could sit for hours and observe the people moving along the adjacent road at my dad's directive. Although the experience of patient waiting was rather discomforting, it taught me to understand and appreciate the different types of people when I was still young. There was a time when I use to feel when the time will come when I will have my own identity and people instead of saying that she is his daughter they will this is so and so, but today I feel proud when people say I manage like my father.

By the time he passed away from a heart attack, I was only 14 years of age. To support the family financially, I was forced to start working at an early age. Devoid of professional skills, I decided to study computer programming. My uncle played a key role in my course as he allowed me to enrol in his institute. I can confidently say that my computer education was the turning point. I became an expert software programming engineer soon after completing my studies. As a result, my entry into the corporate world was rather seamless.

Inside

Starting new business is one thing, but their success and failure depend on the customers and the employees, there are many phases of organization it is important to know in advance the future challenges of an organization for the success of the business, the type of leadership needed in the organization, managing incorporates in personal and entrepreneurial feelings you cannot just go with only systems and models, on the contrary, I would rather say it is deep thinking about the success, your personality, decision-making ability, value and ethics hence the leaders in the organization should also be courageous, committed and loyal.

This book is about the stages of the organization, it pains areas what measure can increase productivity and keep the work culture happy.

Dedication

Life is like a train many people join at the same time many leaves on their station, it is like a journey writing acknowledgement for this is a very tough task, in this 30 years of the journey many were always by side directly or indirectly they have to help me. I would like to thank all of them. It is said enemies are your best friends they teach you the best lessons of your life, I have always appreciated people who have criticized me I have taken their criticism positively I believe they are the real teachers of my life, my sincere thanks to all of them.

I would like to thank all my teachers, professors, friends & my husband.

Few people were real heroes of my life, my all the bosses especially my first boss (MD) what I am today is because of him and my dad, they have taught me the best lessons of life & management.

My princess my daughter has always been a source of motivation for me.

Introduction

Once you enter into corporate life then gone are your college days this is another phase of your life no bunking, sleeping in classes, late-night chats with your friends, sitting on backbenches, arriving late in classes, giving false reasons of not doing homework, etc., in this new world if you reach late no questions asked straightway salary will be cut, no one will excuse for your bad attitude, you cannot lie to anyone this is the corporate world. A completely new rule book of your life.

Earlier you must have heard about corporate life the office politics and the competition and discipline to succeed which many times are taken lightly by the students but the fact is that all these are true and you cannot escape from all of this you can only survive if you accept the reality of this new world "Corporate world" then only you will be able to tackle this.

You have to remember only one rule and that is if you do not perform you are out of this game you have to give you 100 per cent, hard work is the only mantra for success. The truth is that we take the job for fulfilling our dreams, slowly we get involved and start adapting corporate culture.

When you are new you think that productivity, accountability and hard work is the key to success soon you will realize the bitter truth that how the blame game is played for the success, you will come to know how you are blamed where your participation was very less in case of failure, and if it success nobody will bother to give you credit.

We cannot deny the fact of organizational politics. Whether you are professional or the owner of the company you are going through the pain of organizational politics but nobody wants to speak about this bitter taste of life, sometimes the organizational politics is not negative mangers uses this to get the work done, but when the instructions are not communicated properly employees treat this as organizational politics.

Growing is good after all we are working hard for our dreams, but how you should get succeed it depends on your human nature. Office politics is everywhere, and you cannot escape it, but do not get too involved in it otherwise, it will spoil your career.

This book will help the owner of the organization on how she/he can make the workplace better by avoiding a few things. For freshers, it helps in dealing with office politics.

Chapter 1
Stages of organization

Let us understand the phases and changes needs and challenges we face as we grow and why certain things like organization structure, coordination etc., works in certain phases and do not work in certain phases during the development of an organization since the requirement is different for different phase the entrepreneur also have to make changes in their attitude, thought, behaviour and way of thinking towards the growth and organization development.

Like our age, the age of the organization also grows on the assumption that the organization grow and expand each year. These stages will help the business owner understand why certain things like organization structure, coordination etc., works in certain phases and do not work in certain phase during the organizational development. Since different phases require different competencies of the entrepreneur, this will orient towards the strategic policy.

1. When an organization which is like newborn babies where size is small, the structure is informal and employees are loyal flat organization structure and the company is ready to invest.
2. After few years when the company grow at this stage, the functional managers are appointed to control the processes, rules regulation procedures are formalized and standardized, the final control remains in the hand of an entrepreneur only.
3. In this phase, the owner delegates important task to managers they are responsible for achieving the targets and managing their teams here management interference is very less. A division structure is created with separate product groups and individual managers.
4. Here more concentration is on the coordination be-

tween the units because I large organization most of the senior position is taken by headquartering and then the divisional managers work and manage

5. Collaboration amongst line and staff divisions is gone for and this makes a separation of the various levelled coordination structures, for example, a network structure or an undertaking association. This stage is described by much-shared contact between workers utilizing a wide range of conference gatherings. There are little formalization and institutionalization.
6. In this *'growth through undertaking phase'* the organization only requires good external contacts and alliances. These can be found in mergers, alliances, and extensive networks. By providing insight into the growth phases, this can be a tool for organizations to tackle the subsequent growing pains. Organizations will be prepared for any possible growing pains, so they can anticipate them. However, they cannot determine the exact moment growing pains present themselves as it is not possible to determine the duration of a growth phase in advance.

Growing pains can also have a positive effect on a company. These growing pains are experienced as something negative by the parties involved, but essentially, they are an excellent means to shake up the organization and make everyone aware that they must embark on a new course.

The organization has gone through different growth pains. However, they are not linearly related and at the same time if growth pains are not addressed the organization is brought back to the original state. The leadership crises resolution furthers a growth but likely to affect autonomy. The resolution of crises of autonomy will give rise to crises of control. This resolution may progress as the organization grows if there is functional politics which take the organization to high-performance growth however the toxic environment is likely to create an environment of nonperformance. Furthermore, organizational politics do not allow a smooth transition from one stage to another in the process the growth pains get multiplied to come to a stage where there are dysfunctional aspects of politics get magnified.

Chapter 2

Human nature and organization politics

There are multiple dimensions of organizational politics or workplace politics. The first thing that comes in mind is whether human nature is the factor that affects the organization politics?

What is human nature? Human nature is the identity of a person which refers to distinguishing characteristics such as the way of thinking, feeling behaving that human tends to have naturally. Development of human nature depends on many factors such as cultural background, religion, caste, society, family environment, friends, schooling, educational background are some of the factors that are responsible for the creationist.

What is Organizational politics? it refers to a variety of activities associated with the use of influence tactics to improve personal or organizational interests. Studies indicate that individuals with political skills tend to do better in gaining more personal power as well as managing stress and job demands, than their politically naive counterparts. They also have a greater on organizational outcomes Are the politics dysfunctional or normal phenomena? Dysfunctional politics can sink an organization, and yet most of the executives do react with distaste to the idea of being a savvy organizational politician. It appears self-serving and contrary to values and ethics. However, the reality is that politics is normal and human nature is built on it. It is another influencing process along with the norms, formal authority and expertise. Thus, leaders need to understand the forms it can take and how to use it for the well-being of the organization.

Political behaviour is likely to be present but may not be explicit and need to be gleaned from observation. It may be that manager needs to exert a lot of pressure on a team to get things done as given by emphasizing not drop-down approach but based on actionable work items that focus on workflow based on current activity. The current action is constrained by organizational politics. The organizational intern is the outcome of human nature. Sometimes, it may be necessary for employees to work behind the scenes to build coalitions of believers in a new vision to convince others. Whatever may be the context it is important to understand that the root causes of political activities are often scarce resources (including time pressures), social, economic and structural inequalities, and individual personal motivations. Thus, it is not always that politics are dirty and may be necessary to save the organization. If the CEO of an organization is underperforming leading to the closure of the organization, the employees may form a group and become whistle-blowers to save the organization. Organization politics exist in every organization either for functional or for dysfunctional aspects.

The level that political action happens. Political elements might be considered with the individual player and their political attitudes, and these may develop into a group-level phenomenon.

The political landscape is the extent to which the source of power is informal or formal. Making use of influence, relationships and norms is soft power. Whereas hard power is those which are formal and explicit power drawn upon role authority, expertise, directives, and reward and control mechanisms. However, keeping balance in hard & soft power is very important. Soft structure creates anarchy but if everything is hard it may lead to rigidity.

As the organization grows the need and the demand increases, the manpower increases and at the same time there is an increase in the hierarchy. When the personal influence and informal networks are having a higher role. It looks like the wildflowers as it is dynamic and grows naturally, and no one works for it. However, if the wildflowers can grow it can also form a dense mat through which nothing else can grow. In such kind of organizational form, informal networks likely to challenge the legitimate power and the long-term interests of the organization. They may thwart legitimate change efforts for organizational growth. To deal with this wildflower's kind of politics, the manager needs to understand the informal networks at play. Identify the key brokers, as well as the gaps and fill them by personal dialogue with the broker. If the brokers are harming. Effective managers isolate them by developing a counter-narrative.

If this is not controlled it becomes hard like rock It may be described as one that is made with individual interactions and formal sources of authority such as title, role, expertise, or access to resources. It includes political capital that may be attributed to being a member of different committees. Because rocks symbolize stabilizing foundation that keeps an organization steady in times of crisis. However, the sharp edges of hard power may wreck the organizational vision and mission. The sharp edges may be created due to the incompetent person occupying higher ranks.

The further stage we can call it as procedural politics is an amalgamation of formal authority with organizational systems, they are embedded in the rules, structures, policy guidelines, and procedures that form the basis of political activities. The benefits of these rules and procedures are guiding posts against the arbitrary arts of individual-such as charismatic or autocratic persons or leaders. Thus, It's a functional political. The process that uses structures of control systems, incentives, and sanctions that keep the organization in compliance. However, rules and procedures can also lead to the company becoming overly bureaucratic, where rules are used as a political device to become bureaucrat's raj.

The last stage is like forests Organizations have implicit norms, hidden assumptions, and invisible hence it becomes like the forest it provides cover and safety for employees of an organization. It is important to understand the symptoms so that it should not be mistaken for the diverse human nature.

Chapter –3
Diversity in the organization

> When we listen and celebrate what is both common and different, we become a wiser, more inclusive, and better organization. ~**Pat Wadors**

Diversity at the workplace is accepting the employees from different cultural background, value, ethics, age, ethnicity. diversity aggregate the team level construct represents difference among members of an interdependent workgroup concerning specific personal attribute. Diversity is a positive factor in an organization it not only increases the opportunity for the growth, business it adds value in knowledge by gathering various creative thoughts. It provides a distinct advantage in an era when flexibility and creativity are key competitiveness. Conglomeration promotes creativity and amalgamated groups have been shown to produce better solutions to the problem and higher level of critical analysis. When the industries are undergoing tremendous changes for the improvement and betterment systems it is important to find more effective and better ways to operate. Diversity improves the work culture, provides a competitive advantage, buildability to compete in globally and improves the performance, job satisfaction and relationship with multicultural communities, attracting multiple talents and skills.

The organization having varied people with creative and problem-solving skills creates a competitive environment in the organization. Many times when the people join the organization from different culture, background, the language they have different human nature and this leads to friction/complication with the local employees, however, when the organization make sure that they will have a diverse workforce from the very initial stage, they do not face the problem of acceptability. They are forced to keep their personal opinions outside the organization which result in better growth and work culture. Sometimes the organization faces the problem of high turnover, but many times high turnover is good to avoid organization politics. If a person with high calibre joins the organization irrespective of the state, caste, background and performs high and leaves the job early compared to a person who is in the organization for many years with zero output naturally the early employee is beneficial for the organization.

When there is a mix of employees the employees those who are high performers many times creates a sense of insecurity among the employees those who do not wish to perform they just want to be in the organization, in such cases the turnover ratio is less but at the same time productivity is poor, diversification in such cases helps the organization to create competition among the employees and get the output from them with fewer efforts. Same time it is observed that there are certain unknown impediments which lead toward disengagement at the workplace, resulting in high employee turnover, and consequent poor performance of the organization. Because of existing workforce hindering the performance of the other employees. Many psychologists believe that understanding and appreciating the emotions of another person will give the organization a sensible upshot in terms of managing diversity at the workplace. Hence hiring employees with good emotional intelligence or training your employees is EI helps in the smooth functioning of the team. The term diversity may sound small and simple but it is a mix of holding and managing the objectives of the people from different human nature, hence diversity brings significant challenges to the organization and HR plays a vital role in handling the issues about an individual difference arising out of diversity, to support HR top management are equally expected to join the hands in handling such diversified workforce to confront these kinds of challenges, understanding and appreciating each individual's emotions.

In short, workplace diversity is a people issue, focusing on the difference and similarities that people bring to an organization. Globalization crafts workforce diversity in the organization, however, it is blessing and curse both depending on the management style of the organization if accepted it brings creativity and performance in the organization, on another hand, bringing in the diversified workforce is the real challenge for HR as various behavioural dynamics like trust-mistrust, conflict-collaboration sabotage etc get involved.

Chapter 4

Employees generating Toxic work atmosphere

The economy is in deceleration and jobs are scarce. People try hard and use all the personal influences to get a job. There is a survival trait among all of us, however, this survival trait if acquired by an incompetent person is likely to lead to the toxicity in an organization. The survival trait perse is not negative if the person uses it to upgrade and meet the expectations of the organization will not only add in the productivity of the organization but will also help in individual development. If the survival trait is combined with insecurity perception creates a lot of conflicts and unethical behaviour among the employees. Hence to sustain themselves these employees use a battery of techniques.

One such technique is writing letters against peers, superiors, and organizations irrespective of departments and duties. This kind of behaviour is destruction in the working environment and loss of productivity. One question is why it is so pronounced in organizations? It is one of the traits developed from the colonial past. The colonial bosses who have no proper feedback mechanism relied on this form of feedback.

It is natural to have grievances as the resources are limited and individual demands are increasing, moreover, the nonacceptance of people from diverse cultural backgrounds and behaviours also leads to insecurity. This leads to a lack of trust and the formation of mutually destructive groups.

When people work together grievances are expected but to settle the grievance every organization has its respective managers or HR process. Employees can talk or formally complain instead of writing and hurting the dignity of others. The grievances should either pertain to the performance, work environment or compensation. When the grievance is pointing to a person or vilification of the person from another department/ area it is not a grievance but settling of personal petty issues, afraid of not being heard. Less workload or inability to work for their role could also be one of the reasons for such behaviour.

This also indicates that the employee is concerned about her/his insecurity rather than an organizational goal. If these letters are given cognition by the organization, there will be an incentive to write more letters and divert the superior from addressing the goals.

How to organization should address these issues?

This can be addressed by having a strong feedback mechanism.

1. There should be trust in the organization such that genuine professional respect and collegiality should prevail.
2. Managers should be trained to address the departmental issues as and when they arise
3. The anonymous letters should be replied with a message that this will not be entertained, at the same the time it will be treated as unethical behaviour of the employees.
4. Professional ethics shall be inculcated in the employees.
5. Proper design of workload suitable to the persons competent level should be given

Sometimes these letters may not be by their own volition and may be instigated by another person to settle their egos. Superiors should ignore such mutually destructive behaviours and infuse teamwork and belongingness for the betterment of the organization as well as employees.

Chapter 5

A Wrong Man In Workers' Wonderland

There is a smaller margin for error today in hiring and promoting people into key positions, and a greater need to target development efforts to ensure that they make a difference. A bad senior-level hire or promotion can severely damage a company's external brand, affecting customer trust and loyalty, and resulting in lost commercial opportunity. -Brian Clapp

Today where everyone puts their best to get the best. Sometimes management decides to promote the existing to save their cost and time or to motivate their employees which many times turn out to wrong hiring it is like "Placing a wrong person in right place".

When a hired or promoted person do not do their job effectively, the companies productivity goes done also it is the loss of the number of hours companies have spent in training that person. More it demoralises the other employees and they also start stepping down themselves for the cooperation which ultimately limits their productivity creating ripple effects across the team.

Getting a position is difficult; true but to remain/maintain that position is more difficult, unless the leaders have leadership qualities it is very difficult to justify the position, and leadership quality can only be earned by the experience leaders should be courageous, loyal, they should know how? When? And where? To use emotional intelligence in a different way for different people. When the company hires an inexperienced person on the senior position no doubt they successfully close the vacancies, but the situation becomes worst.

Nobody likes getting a move on for somebody who isn't attempting or couldn't care less. The more drawn out your veteran colleagues must force twofold obligation to cover an awful recruit, the more awful confidence will be. Pessimism can fan out quickly, and it won't take long for the assurance of the whole group to sink.

One bad hire can lead to the tremendous which can take months to recover the morale of the employees and productivity losses. The more time the person will remain with you worse will be penalties every day that person is a loss for the company.

What does the company lose in this?

- The person is a misfit in the culture
- Productivity loss
- Increase in rejection / poor quality of work
- No solution only complaints or excuses
- Loss of moral of another employee
- The subordinates will always be dissatisfied
- Increase in organizational politics
- Last but not the least financial losses
- Cost of hiring again

"There was a group of people who worked hard their whole life, GOD kept them separately in one place thinking that since they are hardworking they will do some productive work, and one fine day because of the mistake of gatekeeper one man who never worked in his life entered that group. Because of his inexperience in work he started distracting the worker by building useless things and spoiled everything."

Chapter 6
Leadership Intervention

Transformation is a process, and as life happens there are tons of ups and downs. It's a journey of discovery - there are moments on mountaintops and moments in deep valleys of despair. -Rick Warren

Transformation planning is a process of developing a strategic plan for modifying an enterprise's business process through the modification of policies, procedures and processes to move the organization from an "as is" state to a "to be" state, whereas change management is the process for obtaining the enterprise intelligence to perform transformation planning by assessing an organization's people and cultures to determine how changes in business strategies, organizational design, organization structure, processes, and technology systems will impact the enterprise.

We live in a world which transforms and headway every second when the lifestyle changes there is changes in the expectation and demands of the individuals. This means the market also have to change to meet the demand of the individuals, most of the organizations are successful because they were able to meet the demand of the people/customers they have adapted the changes for their betterment. However, changes are not always an easy method hence it is important to know when the changes are needed or when the company should go for transformation. Any business in the present quick moving condition that is searching for the pace of progress to ease back is probably going to be painfully disillusioned. The world is evolving regularly: the populace is changing, client patterns are changing, innovation is changing, and the economy is evolving. Organizations who neglect to grasp switch can without much of a stretch breeze up as fossils – distant and incapable to contend under current switching conditions. Change is significant for any association fact is, without change, organizations would lose their critical edge and neglect to meet the ever-changing necessities of clients.

The economy can influence relationship in both constructive and destructive ways and both can be upsetting. A strong economy and growing zeal for things and organizations will infer that associations must consider the improvement that may incorporate the progress of staff and new workplaces. These measures offer open doors for staff, yet what's more address, new challenges.

A feeble economy can make appreciably more issues as associations wind up hoping to choose problematic decisions that can influence labourers' pay and benefits and even sabotage their jobs. The ability to manage the two pieces of the deals are essential for affiliations that need to keep up a strong brand and strong rapport with clienteles similarly as delegates.

Change in the organization allows the employees to learn and nurture ultimately the organization also get the advantage because when the employees progress the organization automatically progress it is an indirect relationship, however concocting employees for these changes involve lots of patients and training. Organization need to evaluate the employee's proficiencies and then fill the gaps between current and required skills. Many time recruits point out the area of growth and improvement it is a third party inspection, but existing employees should also be given the same weightage and status.

Chapter 7

Role of Human Resource

> **Neglecting human resources are like a person functioning without a heart.**
>
> **Appreciate the real value of human resources. "Human resources are like natural resources; they're often buried deep. You have to go looking for them; they're not just lying around on the surface." - Ken Robinson**

Conventionally, the payroll, attendance, and other routine HR work were handled by administrative officers, largely debatable was the role of an administrative officer. She/he uses to take care of routine HR activities like shortlisting resume, record keeping, benefits, and other HR-related work.

There is no position for HR professionals in the organization still today many organizations neglect this crucial department thinking it as a waste of money due to a lack of understanding of new reality.

Hence profession is rising due to the changing needs and demands of the competitive market. Their work has shifted more from the back office to organizational transformation, focusing on strategic and business partnerships. Broadly speaking, most human resources leaders focus on building a workforce that reflects their organizational strategic vision. The expansion of the role of HR in organization signifies the progress of HR in the corporate world over the last two decades, compared to the earlier role of administrative function now it is more of a strategic and advisory role based on human capital management.

Because of the involvement of HR inside the organization has resulted in the "Best Practices" in the organization, hence the organization are increasingly considering the Human Resource for the betterment and survival in the competition.

Increasing demand for HR in an organization has incited the organization to make themselves ready for this competitive market and start innovative ideas. The management has started hiring HR to help their organization to move towards the working style of corporate and to develop or recruit skill set that will reflect the image of the organization in a much more modern style workplace and showcase the changing trends in the organization.

HR can be very helpful in the supporting engagement, improving performance levels, and leading transformation efforts. Transformation is the process of accepting the changes for the betterment of an organization, the organization who do not opt for the transformation they find it difficult to meet the demand.

It is important to have teamwork and diversity in culture, for an organization to succeed. No doubt handling manpower in the current scenario has become more challenging than earlier, hiring staff from multi-cultural background for a mix of best skills and cultural adaptability has become a challenge for human resources, but also a big reward in terms of the long-term development of the organization.

Diversity in employees not only creates a healthy work environment but kills the organization politics to a large extent improves the learning process when many employees are hired from the same state or through reference employees tends to form the group and support each other for their survival which later on takes the shape of survival of fittest and ultimately the organization productivity suffers, there are less work and more gossip and it becomes like a hard stalwart to break.

About The Author

Dr Nikhat M Hamza

The author of this book is a tailor-made personality who has consummately blended her 27 years' involvement in different manufacturing Industries like Drip irrigation/ Automobile/ Fabrication/ IT and Education.
She holds an MBA and PhD in Human nature, currently, she is Director Human Resources & Faculty Training Development at one of the University in India

She is an able leader who has spent more than 19 years in a leadership role, which has given her a good understanding of the handling manpower, and the mindset of the people. She plays a strong link between the management and the employees.

Because of extensive research in organizational politics, she not only understands the organization politics but she has expertise in fixing the problem of the organizational politics in the organization which help the organization in increasing the productivity and making the happy workplace environment.

She writes in newspapers, blogs, magazine She is also the founder of "Centre for business coaching and mentoring" this centre works for the transformation of the organization for the better productivity

References

- https://www.toolshero.com/strategy/greiner-growth-model/

www.ingramcontent.com/pod-product-compliance
Lightning Source LLC
Chambersburg PA
CBHW050326220526
45465CB00005B/2149